20 Ways to Cook

MINCED BEEF

Gail Duff

D1338296

Thomas Harmsworth Publishing Company

First Published 1994 by
Thomas Harmsworth Publishing
Company
Old Rectory Offices
Stoke Abbott
Beaminster
Dorset DT8 3JT
United Kingdom

British Library Cataloguing-in-Publication
Data. A catalogue record for this book is
available from the British Library.

ISSN 1355-4050
ISBN 0 948807 20 2

Printed and bound in Great Britain by
BPC Paulton Books Ltd

CONTENTS

INTRODUCTION

Minced beef has been one of the major culinary developments of the twentieth century. From being treated as a curiosity in the late nineteen fifties it has, in its many forms, become the mainstay of the housewife.

Minced beef is always available, it is easy to store and it is one of the cheapest forms of one-hundred per cent edible meat that you can buy. As with all beef cuts, it is an excellent source of protein and provider of iron and vitamin B12.

Open a refrigerator or freezer in most households and you will find minced beef, fresh or frozen, waiting to be made into casseroles or to be topped with potatoes or pastry. It is a marvellous accompaniment to pasta and it can also be flavoured with curry spices to be served with rice. Then there are beef burgers, meatballs, stuffed vegetables and meat loaves. You could eat it every day for weeks without getting bored.

Even in a household that relies to a certain extent on convenience foods, you will still find it in ready-made pies and shepherd's pies, lasagne and beef burgers. How did we ever do without it?

One of the joys of using minced beef is that it literally requires no preparation in order to make it into an excellent meal. There is no chopping, jointing or slicing to be done before putting it into the pan. It can also be cooked in minutes if you need it to be. Of course you can also cook it for longer, cover it with something, or mould it into shapes, but you have to actually do something to other meats before any of this can be done.

Mincemeat is the cook's ally. It is cheap and nutritious, you can take as little, or as much time in the cooking or preparation, and it will make memorable meals.

AVAILABILITY

Fresh minced beef is available all the year round from independent butchers and supermarkets. Frozen minced beef is also available from these sources and can also be found in small grocers' shops.

TYPES AVAILABLE

Minced beef can vary in both the amount of fat that is included with the meat and also in the coarseness of the mince. In general, the leaner you buy it the better. In some cases the leaner types will be labelled as such. If they are not, then look carefully before you buy. The whiter the overall appearance, the more fat was included at the mincing stage.

Some people prefer a coarser mince to others. The coarseness is rarely stated on the packet in supermarkets, so it is a case of looking before you buy, to choose the one that is right for you. Some butchers make up two grades of coarse-

ness when they are preparing mince and may, or may not, advertise the fact. Most supermarket mince is fairly fine. Both types work well for all the recipes in this book. The choice of coarseness is purely a matter of personal taste.

AMOUNT PER SERVING

The amount of mincemeat that you need per person really depends on the type of recipe that you are making. If the dish involves mostly meat with only one or two extra ingredients allow 4 - 6 oz (125 - 175g). If the meat is to be mixed with other ingredients, such as dried beans or breadcrumbs, then you will need 2 - 4 oz (50 - 125g). Meat loaves usually use 1 lb (450g), whereas only 8 oz (225g) is needed to make four pasties.

All the recipes will serve four people even though the meat quantity varies.

STORING AND FREEZING

Where there is no refrigerator or freezer, minced beef should be eaten on the day of purchase and kept, in its wrapper, in a cool place until cooking.

Minced beef will keep in the refrigerator for up to two days. Keep it wrapped.

To freeze minced beef, make sure that it is sealed tightly in a polythene bag or in the plastic-wrapped tray in which it is often bought from supermarkets. Keep minced beef in the freezer for up to three months. Thaw it in the refrigerator.

Ready-made burgers may be kept in the freezer for up to one month.

BASIC PREPARATION

The beauty of using minced beef is that it really requires no preparation before cooking. Make sure that it is broken up well, both before putting it into the pan and directly after. This applies especially to minced beef that has been frozen as it tends to cling together in a lump.

SEASONING

Throughout this book I only mention seasoning where I think it is necessary. Bear in mind that in many recipes the strength of flavour comes from other ingredients and not from the use of salt or pepper.

BASIC COOKING METHODS

Quick Frying

Minced beef can be fried very quickly so that a whole dish can be cooked in a matter of minutes. The result is small pieces of meat that have a slightly chewy texture, rather reminiscent of small pieces of quick-fried steak. The whole process is really a variation on the Chinese method of stir-frying.

Since minced beef contains a certain amount of fat, no additional fat is necessary when you cook using this method. You will need a large, heavy frying pan with a thick base. Heat it on a high heat without any fat and, as soon as it is hot, put in the minced beef. Immediately start to break it up with a spoon and keep stirring so none sticks to the pan. After a short while, you will find that a certain amount of moisture collects in the pan. Keep stirring for this to completely evaporate and for the meat to brown.

(If you find that the surface of your frying pan is not suitable for this method, heat ½ oz (15g) butter or 1 tablespoon oil in the pan before putting in the meat).

Once the meat has browned, put in additional ingredients and flavourings. Chopped garlic and/or onions (particularly spring onions) are more or less essential. Then you can add other ingredients that will cook quickly such as sliced mushrooms or tomatoes, chopped green peppers, courgettes or aubergines, or even slices of orange. Choose chopped fresh or crumbled dried herbs to go with the other ingredients. Parsley used in quantity works exceptionally well. Other flavouring ingredients include Worcestershire sauce, mushroom ketchup, soy sauce, tomato purée or a small amount of red wine or sherry.

You will be able to prepare the whole dish in around 15 minutes.

Casseroling

For a meat dish with a softer, moister texture, add more liquid to the meat and cook it either in the oven or on a low heat on top of the stove.

Begin the process in the same way as for quick frying, using either a large frying pan with a lid or a wide-based saucepan. Lower the heat and put in a chopped medium onion and/or a chopped garlic clove. Similar vegetables as mentioned above can be added or, as the cooking process is longer, chopped or grated root vegetables or celery or other types that need a longer cooking time. Add flavourings and herbs and then ½ pint (275ml) liquid (usually stock or a mixture of stock and a small amount of alcohol such as wine, beer or sherry). Bring the liquid to the boil, cover the pan and simmer for 20 - 30 minutes or until the added vegetables are tender. To cook the same dish in the oven, use a flameproof casserole. Instead of simmering on top of the stove, put the casserole into a preheated 350F/180C/gas 4 oven for 45 mins - 1 hour.

Pie Fillings

For pastry-covered pies or for a cottage or shepherd's pie covered with creamed potatoes, cook the mincemeat on top of the stove as above for 20 minutes. Cool the meat slightly. Put it into an ovenproof dish or pie dish. Cover with the pastry or creamed potato and put the pie into a preheated 400F/200C/gas 6 oven for 20 minutes or until the toppings are golden brown.

For pasties, the mincemeat can be used raw as a filling. In this case cook the pasties at 350F/180C/gas 4 for 45 minutes, covering them with damp greaseproof paper if they brown too quickly.

Microwaving

Using the basic ingredients, flavourings and liquids as for casseroling, mix them into the beef in a large, microwave-proof container. Cover and microwave on high for 15 minutes, stopping after each 5 minutes to break up the meat. Leave to stand for 5 minutes before serving.

Pressure Cooking

Again using similar ingredients, liquids and flavourings as for casseroling, mix them together in the pressure cooker. Put on the lid, bring them up to temperature and cook according to the manufacturer's instructions.

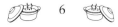

LASAGNE

Lasagne is made by layering pasta leaves with a minced beef mixture and a white sauce that has been flavoured with cheese. More white sauce and cheese are spread over the top of the dish before it is put into the oven to brown. A minced beef mixture for lasagne usually contains onion, garlic, mushrooms and tomatoes or tomato purée, plus a mixture of herbs which often includes basil, oregano and thyme. Cook the beef on top of the stove as for casseroles and put the dish into a preheated 400F / 200C / gas 6 oven for about 20 minutes for the cheese to brown on top.

There are two types of lasagne available, one that needs cooking in salted water first and one that can be used straight from the packet with no previous cooking.

MAKING BEEF BURGERS

For beef burgers, allow 3 - 4 oz (75 - 125g) minced beef per burger. This can be left plain, seasoned only with salt and pepper, or you can add flavourings such as minced onion, crushed garlic, chopped fresh or crumbled dried herbs, or spices such as curry powder, paprika and cayenne pepper. Other additions can include chopped onion, mushrooms, celery or green peppers that have been cooked gently in butter or oil. The meat can be mixed half and half with puréed pulses such as red lentils or red kidney beans.

You can shape beef burgers with your hands but, if you make them often, it is easier to use a burger press. This is small, plastic and inexpensive, and comes with a supply of round, waxed papers which are useful both when pressing the burgers and when storing. A burger press ensures that you will make burgers of an even size and shape. They will also hold together better than those made by hand.

When the burgers are formed, put them onto a flat plate or chopping board and then put them into the refrigerator for at least 30 minutes for them to chill and set into shape.

Burgers are best grilled. Use a conventional grill, a ridged, cast iron grill that goes on top of the gas or hot plate, or cook them on a barbecue. If your conventional grill has a rack constructed of a thin wire grid, cover it with aluminium foil in which you have punched one or two fine holes to let the fat get away. Heat the grill with the rack and foil in place before laying the burgers on it.

A ridged, cast iron grill should be lightly oiled and then heated until it begins to smoke. Lower the heat before starting to cook so that an even temperature is maintained in the metal.

When cooking burgers over a barbecue, use a hinged grill rack which is capable of holding four burgers at once. This makes for easy handling and turning over and prevents the burgers from breaking up and dropping into the fire. Cook the burgers 4 - 6 inches (10 - 15cm) above the hot charcoal.

Cooking times: Beef burgers on a conventional or hinged grill: rare 1½ minutes each side; medium 2½ minutes each side; well done 3½ minutes each side.

Beef burgers on a barbecue: rare 3 - 4 minutes each side; medium 5 - 6 minutes each side; well done 7 - 10 minutes each side.

Serving: Beef burgers can be served in a bun

as a snack or a barbecue meal, or on a plate with jacket potatoes or chips. Rings of raw onion, a relish or a mild spiced mustard make ideal toppings or accompaniments enhancing the flavour.

MEATBALLS

Meatballs can be made from mixtures similar to burgers, and soaked breadcrumbs or puréed pulses can be added to the mixture to give a firmer texture. They always need to be flavoured with herbs and/or spices. 1 lb (450g) mince can be made into 12 - 16 small balls. Meatballs are generally browned first to seal the outside and then added to a casserole of vegetables and/or pulses and cooked either in the oven or on top of the stove.

STUFFED VEGETABLES

The minced beef for stuffed vegetables is usually used raw. It can be mixed with softened onions and garlic, soaked breadcrumbs and a variety of herbs and spices. Marrow rings and beef tomatoes are ideal for stuffing with minced beef.

BEEF STOCK

Wherever stock is mentioned in the following pages as a cooking liquid you can either use a home made stock or a stock cube. If you use a cube, choose one of the better brands that is not heavily flavoured and coloured and which does not contain monosodium glutamate.

To make a natural beef stock. Put a piece of marrow bone into a large, heavy saucepan. Add an onion, halved, and a carrot and celery stick roughly chopped. Set the pan on a low heat, without any fat and let the marrow bone gently brown. Fill the saucepan with water and add 2 teaspoons black peppercorns and either a bouquet garni or 1 tablespoon dried mixed herbs. Bring to the boil, cover and simmer for 1 hour 30 minutes. Strain off the stock, cool it and store it in a covered container in the refrigerator for up to 1 week.

TOMATO AND CELERY RELISH FOR BURGERS

8 oz (225g) tomatoes
2 celery sticks
I medium onion
2 tablespoons olive oil
I garlic clove, crushed
I teaspoon celery seeds (optional)
I tablespoon white wine vinegar
I teaspoon soft brown sugar

Scald, skin and chop the tomatoes. Finely chop the celery and onion. Heat the oil in a saucepan on a low heat. Put in the celery and onion and soften them. Mix in the tomatoes and celery seeds, if using. Add the vinegar and bring to the boil. Stir in the sugar. Cover and cook gently for 2 minutes. Take the pan off the heat and turn the relish into a bowl to cool.

Peeling Tomatoes (the scalding method)
To peel tomatoes, put them into a bowl and pour boiling water over them. Count to ten slowly then drain off the boiling water and immerse the tomatoes in cold water. This stops the tomatoes cooking and, using your fingers, you will be able

to peel the skins away easily.

FLAVOURINGS

Onions and/or garlic are usually essential.

Herbs: Parsley (use as much as you like); sage (use sparingly); thyme; marjoram or oregano; basil (in Italian style dishes); savory (good with root vegetables); chives (in quick-cooked dishes or burgers).

Spices: Paprika and cayenne pepper; curry powder and other curry spices (cumin, coriander); nutmeg, mace and allspice (for an old fashioned flavour).

Cooking liquids: Stock (mix any of the following with stock): tomato juice; tomato and vegetable juice; carrot juice; beer; red wine; sherry.

GLOSSARY

Beef Tomatoes: Large tomatoes, each weighing 4 - 6 oz (125 - 175g), round and flattened slightly from top to bottom. They are ideal for stuffing.

Chili: Small capsicum (related to green and red peppers), 4 - 6 inches (10 - 15cm) long and about ½ inch (1.3cm) thick, tapering to a point. Chilies can be red or green and they have a very hot flavour. To prepare them, remove the core and slit them in half lengthways. With a small, pointed knife, remove all seeds and pith. Finely chop the flesh. Do not rub your eyes or touch your mouth until you have washed your hands.

Flageolet Beans: Small dried beans, similar in size and shape to haricot beans and pale green in colour. They are available dried or tinned.

If unavailable, substitute haricot beans.

Granular Mustard: Mustard prepared with whole mustard grains instead of, or as well as, mustard powder. Granular mustards vary in flavour but tend to be mild and spicy.

Mace: Mace is the outer covering of the nutmeg in the form of a hard, spindly, bright yellow shell. When ground to a yellow powder it has a sharp spicy flavour. It can be used in both sweet and savoury dishes.

Savory: A culinary herb with a dry, savoury flavour. Both an annual summer savory and a perennial winter variety can be grown in temperate climates. Savory can also be bought dried. It is an excellent herb for beef.

Vegetable Suet: A suet produced from palm and other vegetable oils, it is in the form of small, thin pieces of white fat. It can be bought from most supermarkets and grocers' shops.

TABLE OF OVEN TEMPERATURES

	Fahrenheit (F)	Celsius (C)	Gas mark
	150	70	
	175	80	
	200	100	
Very cool	225	110	¼
	250	120	½
	275	140	1
Cool	300	150	2
Warm	325	160	3
Moderate/ Medium	350	180	4

Fairly Hot	375	190	5
	400	200	6
Hot	425	220	7
	450	230	8
Very hot	475	240	9
	500	260	9

IMPERIAL/METRIC CONVERSIONS

Dry weight		Liquid measure	
ounces	grams	fluid ounces	millilitres
1	25	1	25
2	50	2	50
3	75	3	75-90
4 (¼ lb)	125	4	125
5	150	5 (¼ pint)	150
6	175	6	175
7	200	7	200
8 (½ lb)	225	8	225
9	250	9	250
10	275	10 (½ pint)	275
11	300	11	300
12 (¾ lb)	350	12	350
13	375	13	375
14	400	14	400
15	425	15 (¾ pint)	425
16 (1 lb)	450	16	450
17	475	17	475
18	500	18	500
2¼ lb	1000 (1 kilo)	20 (1 pint)	550
		1¾ pints	1000 (1 litre)

SUMMER BEEF SOUP

Serves: 4
Type of dish: hot main course
Suitable for first course: yes, serve in smaller quantities
Preparation time: 40 minutes
Waiting time: nil
Cooking time: 20 minutes
Suitable for dinner parties: as first course
Special equipment: large saucepan
Suitable for microwave cooking: yes
Suitable for pressure cooking: yes
Suitable for freezing: yes
Calorie content: medium
Carbohydrate content: low
Fibre content: low
Protein content: high
Fat content: medium

8 oz (225g) French beans
12 oz (350g) small courgettes
1 lb (450g) tomatoes
1 large onion
1 garlic clove
4 tablespoons olive or sunflower oil
1½ lb (675g) minced beef
2 pints (1.15 litres) stock
¼ pint (150ml) dry white wine (or use all stock)
1 tablespoon chopped basil (or 1 teaspoon dried)
1 tablespoon chopped thyme (or 1 teaspoon dried)
1 tablespoon chopped marjoram (or 1 teaspoon dried)
salt and freshly ground black pepper
4 tablespoons grated Parmesan cheese

Top and tail and finely chop the French beans. Wipe and thinly slice the courgettes. Scald, skin and roughly chop the tomatoes. Finely chop the onion and garlic.

In a large saucepan, soften the onion and garlic in the oil on a low heat. Raise the heat to medium and put in the beef. Break it up well and stir it about until it browns. Mix in the beans, courgettes and tomatoes. Pour in the stock and bring it to the boil. Add the wine, if using, plus the herbs and seasonings. Cover and simmer for 20 minutes.

To serve, either pour the soup into one large tureen or into four individual bowls and scatter the Parmesan cheese over the top.

☆   ☆   ☆

Chef's tips:

☆ If you are serving the soup as a main meal, use large, deep bowls for serving.

☆ Accompany the main meal with crusty bread and a side salad that can be eaten either with the soup or afterwards.

☆ The soup makes a good first course before a light salad meal or one based on vegetarian ingredients (to non-vegetarians, of course).

☆ When buying ingredients for the soup, choose small courgettes, no more than 1 inch (2.5cm) in diameter.

☆ The Parmesan can be replaced by ½ oz (15g) grated Cheddar cheese per serving.

☆ To freeze, omit the cheese. Cool the soup completely and transfer it to a rigid, plastic container. Cover it and store it for up to one month. Thaw the soup in the refrigerator and reheat it gently in a saucepan.

BEEF AND HARICOT BEAN SOUP

Serves: 4
Type of dish: hot main course
Suitable for first course: in small quantities
Preparation time: 30 minutes
Waiting time: nil
Cooking time: 1 hour 30 minutes
Suitable for dinner parties: as first course
Special equipment: large saucepan
Suitable for microwave cooking: yes
Suitable for pressure cooking: yes
Suitable for freezing: yes
Calorie content: medium
Carbohydrate content: medium
Fibre content: medium
Protein content: high
Fat content: medium

 18

6 oz (175g) haricot beans	
1 lb (450g) minced beef	
12 oz (350g) carrots	
8 oz (225g) mushrooms	
4 celery sticks	
2 red peppers	
2 large onions	
4 tablespoons olive or sunflower oil	
1 garlic clove, finely chopped	
one 14 oz (400g) tin tomatoes in juice	
2 tablespoons dried mixed herbs	
1 garlic clove, crushed with pinch salt	
freshly ground black pepper	
4 pints (2.15 litres) stock	
salt	

Put the haricot beans into a small saucepan and cover them with cold water. Bring them to the boil and boil them for 10 minutes. Drain them.

Finely chop the carrots, mushrooms and celery sticks. Core the peppers, remove the seeds and pith and dice the flesh. Finely chop the onions. In a food processor or blender, liquidise the tomatoes with their juice.

Heat the oil in a large saucepan on a low heat. Put in the onion and chopped garlic and soften them. Raise the heat. Put in the beef, break it up well and stir it until it browns.

Put the vegetables into the pan. Pour in the liquidised tomatoes. Add the herbs, crushed garlic, black pepper and stock.

Bring the soup to the boil on a medium heat. Cover and simmer it gently for 1 hour 30 minutes, or until the beans are soft. Add salt to taste.

Chef's tips:
☆ Serve in big, deep bowls.
☆ Chopped parsley or grated Parmesan or Cheddar cheese may be scattered over the top.
☆ Boiling dried beans rapidly for 10 minutes takes the place of a long soaking time in cold water. Since the outer skin of dried beans tends to toughen if cooked in salted water, the salt is added at the end of the cooking time.
☆ To freeze, cool the soup completely and pour it into a rigid, plastic container. Cover it and store it for up to one month. Thaw in the refrigerator and reheat it gently in a saucepan.

BEEF AND CHICKEN LIVER PATÉ

Serves: 4
Type of dish: cold first course
Suitable for main course: yes, served as a salad
   meal
Preparation time: 50 minutes
Cooking time: included in preparation time
Waiting time: 2 hours to chill
Suitable for dinner parties: yes
Special equipment: heavy frying pan, earthen-
   ware dish or terrine
Suitable for microwave cooking: yes
Suitable for pressure cooking: no
Suitable for freezing: yes
Calorie content: high
Carbohydrate content: low
Fibre content: low
Protein content: high
Fat content: high

| 4 oz (125g) chicken livers |
| 2 oz (50g) lean bacon |
| 1 oz (25g) butter |
| 1 medium onion, finely chopped |
| 1 garlic clove, finely chopped |
| 8 oz (225g) minced beef |
| 1 oz (25g) grated cooking apple |
| 6 chopped sage leaves, or 1 teaspoon dried sage |
| freshly-ground black pepper |

Trim the chicken livers of any stringy pieces or discoloured patches. Chop the livers finely. Chop the bacon.

Melt the butter in a heavy frying pan on a low heat. Put in the onion and garlic and soften them. Put in the livers, bacon and beef and cook them gently together for 15 minutes, stirring occasionally. Cool them slightly and add the apple, sage and pepper. Either put the mixture through the fine blade of a mincer or work it in a food processor or blender. Put the mixture into a bowl and beat it well.

Pile the mixture into a small earthenware terrine or dish. Cover it and chill it until it is firm, about 2 hours. Bring the paté out of the refrigerator about 30 minutes before serving to bring it to room temperature.

Chef's tips:
☆ To serve, cut the paté into wedges or slices in the dish, remove them and lay them on individual plates garnished with small pieces of salad.
☆ Toast makes a good accompaniment, cut very thin for a dinner party first course, or more chunkily for a family meal.
☆ To freeze, make sure that the paté is packed into a freezer-proof bowl. You can use a plastic bowl instead of earthenware. Cover the paté and cool it completely before putting it into the freezer. Store for up to one month. Thaw in the refrigerator and bring to room temperature before serving.

QUICK MINCED BEEF WITH LEEKS AND WATERCRESS

Serves: 4
Type of dish: Hot main course
Suitable for first course: no
Preparation time (beef): 40 minutes
Waiting time: nil
Cooking time: included in preparation time
Preparation time (potatoes): 15 minutes
Cooking time (potatoes): 20 minutes
Suitable for dinner parties: no
Special equipment: large, heavy frying pan
Suitable for microwave cooking: no
Suitable for pressure cooking: no
Suitable for freezing: no
Calorie content: high
Carbohydrate content: low
Fibre content: low
Protein content: high
Fat content: high

6 oz (175g) leeks
1 bunch watercress
1½ lb (675g) minced beef
1 garlic clove, finely chopped
1 tablespoon tomato purée
2 teaspoons granular mustard
potato accompaniment (optional):
1½ lb (675g) potatoes
1 oz (25g) butter
1 medium onion, thinly sliced
2 tablespoons tomato purée
1 teaspoon granular mustard
½ pint (275ml) stock
pinch salt

Slice the leeks in half lengthways. Wash them well and thinly slice them. Chop the watercress, removing the thicker stalks.

Heat a large, heavy frying pan on a high heat with no fat. Put in the meat and break it up well. Stir it rapidly so that it does not stick and it browns evenly. Keep stirring until any moisture that collects has evaporated. Put in the garlic and continue to cook until the meat has browned well. Mix in the leeks and cook for 1 minute. Mix in the watercress, tomato purée and mustard. Let the cress heat through and serve as soon as you can.

If you are serving the *potato accompaniment*, it should be begun before the beef is cooked. Peel the potatoes. Melt the butter in a large saucepan. Put in the onion and soften it. Stir in the tomato purée and mustard. Mix in the potatoes. Pour in the stock and bring it to the boil. Add the salt. Cover and cook gently for 20 minutes, or until the potatoes are soft and the liquid has evaporated to make a small amount of sauce.

Chef's tips:
☆ The leeks and watercress should remain fresh-looking and bright green, so no garnish is necessary.
☆ Serve with a contrasting vegetable such as carrots.
☆ Plainly-boiled potatoes or rice can be served instead of the potato accompaniment.

QUICK-FRIED BEEF
WITH PEANUTS

Serves: 4
Type of dish: Hot main course
Suitable for first course: no
Preparation time (beef): 40 minutes
Waiting time: nil
Cooking time: included in preparation time
Preparation time (rice): 15 minutes
Cooking time (rice): 40 minutes
Suitable for dinner parties: yes
Special equipment: large, heavy frying pan
Suitable for microwave cooking: no
Suitable for pressure cooking: no
Suitable for freezing: no
Calorie content: high
Carbohydrate content: low
Fibre content: medium
Protein content: high
Fat content: high

1 small head celery
1 tablespoon crunchy peanut butter
¼ pint (150ml) tomato juice
1 garlic clove, crushed with pinch salt
pinch cayenne pepper
2 large oranges
2 tablespoons sunflower or groundnut oil
1 large onion, finely chopped
2 oz (50g) shelled, unroasted peanuts
1 lb (450g) minced beef

rice accompaniment (optional):
8 oz (225g) long grain brown rice
3 tablespoons olive or sunflower oil
1 medium onion, finely chopped
1 garlic clove, finely chopped
¼ teaspoon cayenne pepper
1 teaspoon paprika
1 pint (550ml) stock
½ teaspoon salt

If you are serving the *rice accompaniment*, begin to cook it before you start the beef recipe. Heat the oil in a saucepan on a low heat. Put in the onion and garlic and soften them. Stir in the cayenne pepper and paprika. Cook them for 1 minute. Stir in the rice. Pour in the stock and bring it to the boil. Add the salt. Cover and simmer for 40 minutes or until the rice is tender and all the liquid has been absorbed.

While the rice is cooking, finely chop the celery. Mix together the peanut butter, tomato juice, garlic and cayenne pepper. Cut the rind and pith from the oranges. Quarter the flesh lengthways and cut it into thin slices.

Heat the oil in a large, heavy frying pan on a high heat. Put in the onion, celery and peanuts and stir-fry them for 2 minutes, or until the onion and celery begin to look transparent. Add the beef, break it up well and stir it until it has browned. Lower the heat and cook for 2 minutes more, stirring occasionally.

Pour in the peanut butter mixture and bring it to the boil. Mix in the oranges and stir for 1 minute to heat them through. Serve immediately so the oranges stay fresh-looking.

Chef's tips:
☆ Serve the beef surrounded by the rice.
☆ Plainly-boiled rice can be served instead of the rice in the recipe.
☆ Because of the celery in the dish you will probably not need another vegetable. However, a green salad makes a good contrast.

CORN, BEEF AND PEPPERS

Serves: 4
Type of dish: Hot main course
Suitable for first course: no
Preparation time (beef): 30 minutes
Waiting time: nil
Cooking time (beef): 40 minutes
Preparation time (rice): 10 minutes
Cooking time (rice): 40 minutes
Suitable for dinner parties: no
Special equipment: large, heavy saucepan
Suitable for microwave cooking: yes
Suitable for pressure cooking: yes
Suitable for freezing: yes
Calorie content: high
Carbohydrate content: medium
Fibre content: medium
Protein content: high
Fat content: medium

One 12 oz (340g) tin sweetcorn
1 red pepper
1 green pepper
4 green chilies
1 lb ripe tomatoes
2 medium onions
4 tablespoons olive or sunflower oil
1 garlic clove, finely chopped
1½ lb (675g) minced beef
2 teaspoons paprika
3 tablespoons chopped parsley
rice accompaniment (optional):
8 oz (225g) long grain brown rice
3 tablespoons olive or sunflower oil
1 small onion, finely chopped
1 garlic clove, finely chopped
1 pint (550ml) stock
½ teaspoon salt
8 oz (225g) tomatoes
2 tablespoons chopped parsley

Drain the sweetcorn. Core the peppers, remove the seeds and pith; finely chop the flesh. Core and finely chop the chilies. Scald, skin and chop the tomatoes. Finely chop the onion.

Heat the oil in a large, heavy saucepan on a low heat. Put in the onion and garlic and soften them. Raise the heat to medium. Put in the beef and break it up well. Stir it until it is brown. Stir in the tomatoes, corn, peppers, chilies, paprika and parsley. Cover the pan and simmer the beef on a low heat for 40 minutes.

For the *rice accompaniment,* heat the oil in a large saucepan on a low heat. Put in the onion and garlic and soften them. Pour in the stock and bring it to the boil. Cover and cook gently for 40 minutes, or until the rice is tender and all the water has been absorbed. While the rice is cooking, chop the tomatoes. Mix them into the rice with the parsley. Cover the rice again and leave it to stand for 5 minutes for the tomatoes to heat through.

☆   ☆   ☆

Chef's tips:

☆ Plainly-boiled or jacket potatoes or plainly-cooked rice can be served instead of the rice given above.

☆ Extra parsley sprigs can be used to garnish, if wished.

☆ If possible, use the variety of sweetcorn that has been canned without the addition of salt and sugar.

☆ To freeze, cool completely and put into a rigid plastic container. Cover and store for up to one month. Thaw in the refrigerator and re-heat gently in a saucepan. The rice can be frozen in a separate container. Thaw it in the refrigerator. To reheat, heat a little oil in a saucepan on a low heat. Stir in the rice, cover and leave on the low heat for 5 minutes.

BEEF, BACON AND CABBAGE IN A POT

Serves: 4
Type of dish: Hot main course
Suitable for first course: no
Preparation time: 25 minutes
Waiting time: nil
Cooking time: 25 minutes
Preparation time (potatoes): 15 minutes
Cooking time (potatoes): 20 minutes
Suitable for dinner parties: no
Special equipment: large, heavy saucepan
Suitable for microwave cooking: yes
Suitable for pressure cooking: yes
Suitable for freezing: yes
Calorie content: high
Carbohydrate content: medium
Fibre content: medium
Protein content: high
Fat content: medium

6 oz (175g) lean unsmoked bacon
1 small-medium sized green cabbage
1 large onion
½ oz (15g) butter
12 oz (350g) minced beef
1 tablespoon spiced granular mustard
6 chopped sage leaves, or 1 teaspoon dried sage
¼ pint (150ml) dry cider
3 oz (75g) Cheddar cheese, grated

potato accompaniment (optional):
1½ lb (675g) potatoes
1 small onion
1 oz (25g) butter
1 teaspoon mustard powder
½ pint (275ml) stock
4 sage leaves, finely chopped
pinch salt

Dice the bacon, shred the cabbage and thinly slice the onion.

Melt the butter in a large, heavy saucepan on a high heat. Put in the beef and bacon and stir them until the beef browns. Mix in the onion, lower the heat and cook for 2 minutes more, stirring occasionally. Mix in the cabbage, mustard, sage and cider. Cover the saucepan and cook the beef on a low heat for 25 minutes, by which time most of the liquid should have evaporated.

Turn the beef and cabbage onto a large serving dish and scatter the cheese over the top.

For the *potato accompaniment*, peel the potatoes and thinly slice the onion. Melt the butter in a saucepan on a low heat. Put in the onion and soften it. Stir in the potatoes and scatter in the mustard. Turn the potatoes until the mustard is evenly distributed over them. Pour in the stock and bring it to the boil. Add the sage and salt. Cover and cook gently for 20 minutes or until the potatoes are soft and the liquid evaporated to a small amount.

☆   ☆   ☆

Chef's tips:

☆ Plainly-cooked potatoes can be served instead of the above accompaniment.

☆ Although the cabbage will shrink as it cooks, make sure that the saucepan that you use is large enough to take the cabbage when it is first put into the pan.

☆ To freeze, cool completely and put into a rigid plastic container. Cover and store for up to one month. Thaw in the refrigerator and reheat gently in a saucepan. The potatoes can be frozen in a separate container, thawed in the refrigerator and reheated gently in a saucepan.

LASAGNE IN A CASSEROLE

Serves: 4
Type of dish: Hot main course
Suitable for first course: no
1st preparation time: 30 minutes
Waiting time: nil
Cooking time: 1 hour
2nd preparation time: 10 minutes
Suitable for dinner parties: no
Special equipment: large casserole with lid; oven
Suitable for microwave cooking: yes
Suitable for pressure cooking: no
Suitable for freezing: yes
Calorie content: high
Carbohydrate content: medium
Fibre content: medium
Protein content: high
Fat content: high

1 lb (450g) tomatoes
4 oz (125g) open mushrooms
1 large onion
3 tablespoons olive or sunflower oil
1 garlic clove, finely chopped
1 lb (450g) minced beef
2 teaspoons dried mixed herbs, or Italian seasoning
8 oz (225g) wholewheat lasagne
½ pint (275ml) stock
cheese sauce:
1 oz (25g) butter
2 tablespoons flour
½ pint (275ml) milk
3 oz (75g) Cheddar cheese, grated

Heat the oven to 350F/180C/gas 4. Scald, skin and chop the tomatoes. Thinly slice the mushrooms and onion. Heat the oil in a large saucepan on a low heat. Put in the onion and garlic and soften them. Raise the heat. Put in the beef and break it up well. Stir it until it browns. Add the tomatoes, mushrooms and herbs. Cook for 2 minutes and take the pan from the heat.

Put one third of the lasagne strips in a single layer in the bottom of a large, flameproof casserole. Put in one third of the beef mixture. Repeat these two layers twice more. Put the casserole on top of the stove on a medium heat. Pour in the stock and bring it to the boil. (*Note:* if your casserole is not flameproof, do not put it directly onto the heat. Instead, bring the stock to the boil before pouring it into the casserole). Cover the casserole and put it into the oven for 40 minutes.

For the *cheese sauce*, put the butter, flour and milk into a saucepan and stir them on a medium heat until they boil and make a thick sauce. Take the pan from the heat and beat in two thirds of the cheese.

Spoon the cheese sauce over the top of the lasagne and scatter the remaining grated cheese over the top. Return the casserole to the oven, uncovered, for 20 minutes.

Chef's tips:

☆ Serve the lasagne directly from the casserole.

☆ A salad or a cooked vegetable such as peas, mange tout peas, French beans or courgettes.

☆ Small portions of the lasagne can be frozen separately in either plastic or foil containers with lids. Store them for up to one month. Reheat them in a medium oven from frozen, transferring from the plastic containers into ovenproof containers beforehand.

MINCED BEEF, BROCCOLI AND FLAGEOLET BEANS LAYERED WITH PASTA

Serves: 4
Type of dish: Hot main course
Suitable for first course: no
Preparation time: 40 minutes
Waiting time: nil
Cooking time: 20 minutes
Suitable for dinner parties: no
Special equipment: deep, ovenproof dish
Suitable for microwave cooking: yes
Suitable for pressure cooking: no
Suitable for freezing: yes
Calorie content: high
Carbohydrate content: medium
Fibre content: medium
Protein content: high
Fat content: high

I lb (450g) broccoli
4 oz (125g) button mushrooms
I medium onion
1½ oz (40g) butter
8 oz (225g) minced beef
½ pint (275ml) stock
8 oz (225g) flageolet beans, soaked and cooked, or one 14 oz (400g) tin flageolet beans, drained
I tablespoon chopped thyme, or I teaspoon dried
I tablespoon chopped marjoram, or I teaspoon dried
8 oz (225g) wholewheat pasta shapes
¾ pint (425ml) milk
2 tablespoons flour
3 oz (75g) Cheddar cheese, grated

Heat the oven to 400F / 200C / gas 6. Cut the broccoli into small florets. Thinly slice the mushrooms and the onion.

Melt half the butter in a large saucepan. Put in the beef, break it up well and stir until it browns. Lower the heat and put in the mushrooms and onion. Cook them for 2 minutes, stirring. Pour in the stock and bring it to the boil. Add the broccoli, beans and herbs. Cover and simmer for 20 minutes.

Cook the pasta in lightly-salted boiling water for 7 minutes or until it is just tender. Drain it.

For the *sauce*, put the remaining butter, the milk and the flour into a saucepan and stir them on a medium heat until they boil and make a thick sauce. Take the pan from the heat and beat

in two thirds of the cheese.

Put one third of the pasta into the bottom of a deep, ovenproof dish, then half the meat and one third of the sauce. Repeat these layers once and then finish with the pasta and the remaining sauce. Scatter the remaining cheese over the top. Put the dish into the oven for 20 minutes, or until the top of the sauce has browned.

☆   ☆   ☆

Chef's tips:
☆ Serve directly from the dish.
☆ No accompaniment is needed, but a salad makes a refreshing contrast.
☆ The meat and pasta may be frozen directly

 45

in the dish, provided that the dish is suitable. Cool the food and dish completely before putting them into the freezer. Store for up to one month. Reheat directly from frozen.

YOGHURT BURGERS WITH TOMATO AND RED PEPPER RELISH

Serves: 4
Type of dish: Hot main course
Preparation time: 30 minutes
Waiting time: 30 minutes
Cooking time: 7 - 10 minutes
Suitable for dinner parties: yes
Special equipment: burger maker; grill or barbecue
Suitable for microwave cooking: with browner
Suitable for pressure cooking: no
Suitable for freezing: yes, before cooking
Calorie content: high
Carbohydrate content: low
Fibre content: low
Protein content: high
Fat content: high

1½ lb (675g) minced beef
4 fl oz (125ml) natural yoghurt
1 garlic clove, crushed with pinch salt
freshly ground black pepper
4 tablespoons chopped parsley
3 tablespoons chopped mint, or 2 teaspoons dried
3 tablespoons chopped chives, or 1 tablespoons dried
relish:
8 oz (225g) tomatoes
2 red peppers
1 medium onion
2 tablespoons olive or sunflower oil
3 tablespoons white wine vinegar
1 teaspoon molasses or black treacle or dark soft brown sugar

Put the beef into a bowl. Beat the yoghurt with the garlic and pepper and mix them into the beef, together with the herbs. Beat well, so the mixture becomes quite smooth.

Divide the mixture into eight portions and make them into round, flat burgers. Leave them in a cool place for 30 minutes to set into shape.

To make the *relish,* scald, skin, seed and finely chop the tomatoes. Core, seed and finely chop the peppers. Finely chop the onion. Heat the oil in a saucepan on a low heat. Put in the onion and cook it until it is transparent. Mix in the tomatoes and red peppers. Add the vinegar and let the mixture boil. Stir in the molasses. Take the pan from the heat and put the relish into a bowl. Cool it completely before serving.

To cook the burgers, heat the grill to high and, if you have an open, wire rack, cover it with foil. Grill the burgers until they are cooked through and brown on both sides, about 7 minutes altogether.

Chef's tips:

☆ To cook on a barbecue, place over hot coals for 5 - 10 minutes on each side, depending on whether rare, medium or well-done is required.

☆ For a snack meal, serve each burger separately in a bun.

☆ For a main meal, serve the burgers with a salad and either jacket potatoes or chips.

☆ Unsuitable for freezing when cooked but, provided that the meat has not been previously frozen, the made burgers can be frozen before cooking and stored ready-made. Stack them in fours with rounds of waxed paper in between them and seal the stacks in separate sealed polythene bags. Store for up to one month. Thaw in the refrigerator before cooking.

RESHMI OMELET

Serves: 4
Type of dish: Hot main course
Suitable for first course: serve half quantities
Preparation time: 30 minutes
Waiting time: 30 minutes
Cooking time: 30 minutes
Suitable for dinner parties: yes
Special equipment: grill, frying pan
Suitable for microwave cooking: with browner
Suitable for pressure cooking: no
Suitable for freezing: yes, uncooked
Calorie content: high
Carbohydrate content: low
Fibre content: low
Protein content: high
Fat content: high

1 lb (450g) minced beef
2 oz (50g) butter
1 medium onion, finely chopped
1 garlic clove, finely chopped
2 teaspoons hot Madras curry powder
1 teaspoon ground cumin
1 teaspoon ground coriander
1 tablespoon tomato purée
4 eggs
4 tablespoons chopped mixed fresh herbs, or 1 tablespoon dried
1 lemon, cut into wedges
1 medium onion, cut into rings

Put the beef into a large mixing bowl. Melt half the butter in a small frying pan on a low heat. Put in the onion and garlic and soften them. Mix them into the beef with the spices and tomato purée. Beat everything well until the mixture is almost smooth. Divide the mixture into eight pieces and shape them into round, flat cakes each about ½ inch (1.3cm) thick. Put them onto a flat plate and chill them for 30 minutes so they set into shape.

Heat the grill to high and, if you have an open wire rack, cover it with foil. Grill the meat cakes for about 4 minutes each side. Keep them warm. Beat each egg separately with 1 tablespoon of the fresh herbs or one quarter of the dried. In an omelet pan, melt half the remaining butter on a low heat. When the foam subsides, put in one of the eggs and spread it over the pan as much as possible, to make a thin, wide omelet. When it

is half set, put two of the meat cakes on top so they sink a little into the egg. When the egg is brown underneath, lift up the omelet and the meat cakes together, using a fish slice or palette knife. Put them, omelet side up, onto a warm individual plate. Cook the rest of the eggs in the same way.

☆   ☆   ☆

Chef's tips:
☆ Serve garnished with the lemon wedges and rings of raw onion.
☆ Serve with a salad and a curry-flavoured

rice.

☆ The meat cakes can be frozen before they are cooked. Stack them in fours with rings of waxed paper in between. Seal each stack of four in a polythene bag. Store for up to one month. Thaw, before cooking, in the refrigerator.

BEEF BURGERS WITH ORANGE

Serves: 4
Type of dish: Hot main course
Suitable for first course: no
Preparation time: 20 minutes
Waiting time: 30 minutes
Cooking time: 10 - 15 minutes
Suitable for dinner parties: yes
Special equipment: grill
Suitable for microwave cooking: with browner
Suitable for pressure cooking: no
Suitable for freezing: yes, uncooked
Calorie content: high
Carbohydrate content: low
Fibre content: low
Protein content: high
Fat content: high

1½ lb (675g) minced beef
1 oz (25g) butter
1 medium onion, finely chopped
1 garlic clove, finely chopped
2 small oranges
1 tablespoon chopped thyme, or 1 teaspoon dried
pinch salt
freshly ground black pepper
1 tablespoon grated Parmesan cheese

Put the beef into a mixing bowl. Heat the butter in a small frying pan on a low heat. Put in the onion and garlic and soften them. Mix them into the beef. Grate the rind of one of the oranges into the beef. Add the thyme and seasonings. Form the mixture into twelve flat cakes each about ½ inch (1.3cm) thick. Put them onto flat plates and refrigerate them for 30 minutes so they set into shape.

Cut the rind and pith from the remaining orange and the pith from the first orange. Cut each orange into six slices.

Heat the grill to high and, if you have an open wire rack, cover it with foil. Lay the burgers on the hot rack and grill them until they are cooked through and browned on each side (about 7 minutes). Lay a slice of orange on each one and sprinkle the cheese on top. Return the grill pan to the heat to brown the cheese.

☆　　☆　　☆

Chef's tips:
☆ Serve with a salad and chips, sautéed potatoes or jacket potatoes.
☆ The burgers can be frozen before cooking.
Put them into stacks of four with waxed paper
in between. Put the stacks into sealed polythene bags and store them for up to one
month. Thaw them in the refrigerator before
cooking.

SPICED SUPER BURGER

Serves: 4, or more if one of several dishes

Type of dish: Hot main course or barbecue party food

Suitable for first course: no

Preparation time: 40 minutes

Waiting time: 2 hours 30 minutes

Cooking time: 25 minutes — loaf; 20 minutes — burger

Suitable for dinner parties: yes

Special equipment: hinged grill suitable for using on a barbecue

Suitable for microwave cooking: with browner

Suitable for pressure cooking: no

Suitable for freezing: yes, before cooking

Calorie content: high

Carbohydrate content: medium

Fibre content: medium

Protein content: high

Fat content: medium

 58

1¼ lb (575g) minced beef
½ small onion
1 garlic clove, crushed
2 tablespoons natural yoghurt
1 tablespoon chopped thyme, or 1 teaspoon dried
3 sage leaves, chopped, or ½ teaspoon dried
1 teaspoon ground cinnamon
sauce:
¼ pint (150ml) natural yoghurt
2 tablespoons tomato purée
1 garlic clove, crushed
½ teaspoon ground cinnamon
loaf:
½ oz (15g) fresh yeast or 2 teaspoons dried
¼ pint (150ml) warm water
1 teaspoon honey, if using dried yeast
8 oz (225g) wholemeal flour
1 teaspoon salt
1 teaspoon cumin seeds
1 teaspoon ground coriander
4 tablespoons olive oil
(alternatively, buy an 8 inch (20cm) diameter flat loaf)

For the *loaf*, sprinkle the yeast into the warm water, adding the honey if you are using dried yeast. Leave the mixture in a warm place for 20 minutes. Put the flour into a bowl with the salt and spices. Make a well in the centre. Pour in the yeast and oil. Mix everything to a dough and knead it on a floured work surface until it is smooth. Return the dough to the bowl, cover it with a clean cloth and leave it in a warm place for 1 hour to double in size.

Heat the oven to 400F / 200C / gas 6. Knead the dough again. Roll it out to an 8 inch (20cm) diameter round and put it into an oiled cake tin of the same size. Leave it in a warm place for 20 minutes.

Bake the loaf for 25 minutes or until it sounds hollow when tapped. Turn it onto a wire rack and let it cool.

While the dough is rising, put the beef into a bowl. Grate the onion into it. Add the garlic, yoghurt, herbs and cinnamon and mix well. Press the mixture into a 7 inch (18cm) diameter cake tin and refrigerate it for 2 hours so it sets into shape. Take it into room temperature for 30 minutes.

For the *sauce*, mix together the yoghurt, tomato purée, garlic and cinnamon.

To cook the burger, place it in the hinged grill. If you are using an ordinary grill, heat it to high and cook the burger for about 8 minutes on each side. On a barbecue, cook the burger 4 - 6 inches (10 - 15cm) over hot coals, again for about 8 minutes on each side, or until it is golden brown and cooked through.

Chef's tips:

☆ To serve, split the loaf in half and put the burger inside. Cut the loaf and burger into wedges and serve the sauce separately.

☆ Serve with a salad. Potatoes may or may not be necessary.

☆ The burger can be frozen before cooking. Chill it first to set it into shape. Turn it out of the cake tin and freeze it on a flat tray. Once frozen, take it off the tray and wrap it in polythene. Store for up to one month. Thaw in the refrigerator. The bread can be cooked and frozen separately. Cool it completely, wrap it in plastic film or put it into a polythene bag. Store for up to two months.

MEATBALLS WRAPPED IN SPINACH LEAVES

Serves: 4
Type of dish: Hot main course
Suitable for first course: no
Preparation time: 30 minutes
Waiting time: nil
Cooking time: 45 minutes
Suitable for dinner parties: yes
Special equipment: casserole with lid
Suitable for microwave cooking: yes
Suitable for pressure cooking: yes
Suitable for freezing: yes
Calorie content: high
Carbohydrate content: low
Fibre content: low
Protein content: high
Fat content: high

1½ lb (675g) minced beef
1 oz (25g) butter
1 medium onion, finely chopped
2 tablespoons chopped parsley
2 tablespoons chopped marjoram, or 2 teaspoons dried
2 tablespoons chopped thyme, or 2 teaspoons dried
¼ teaspoon ground mace
¼ nutmeg, grated
salt and freshly ground black pepper
24 large spinach leaves
½ pint (275ml) stock
rice:
8 oz (225g) long grain brown rice
½ oz (15g) butter
1 small onion, finely chopped
6 spinach leaves, finely chopped
1 pint (550ml) stock
½ teaspoon salt
4 tablespoons chopped parsley

Heat the oven to 400F/200C/gas 6. Put the beef into an bowl. Melt the butter in a small frying pan on a low heat. Put in the onion and soften it. Mix it into the beef with the herbs, mace, nutmeg and seasonings.

With your hands, form the mixture into 12 small balls and wrap each one in two of the spinach leaves. Pack the meatballs into a casserole and pour in the stock. Season again.

Set the casserole on top of the stove on a medium heat and bring the stock to the boil. Cover

the casserole and put it into the oven for 45 minutes.

For the *rice,* melt the butter in a saucepan on a
low heat. Put in the onion and soften it. Shred
the spinach leaves and stir them into the onion.
Stir in the rice. Pour in the stock and bring it to
the boil. Add the salt. Cover and simmer for 40
minutes or until the rice is tender and all the
stock absorbed. Fork in the parsley.

Chef's tips:

☆ Serve the meatballs on a bed of rice either on a serving dish or on individual plates.

☆ Serve with a vegetable that contrasts in colour such as carrots or tomatoes.

☆ To freeze before cooking, shape the meatballs but do not wrap them. Freeze them separately on a tray and then pack them into a sealed polythene bag. Store them for up to one month. Thaw them in the refrigerator. To freeze after cooking, cool the meatballs completely and pack them into a rigid plastic container with any cooking liquid. Cover them. Store them for up to one month. Reheat from frozen. Transfer the meatballs to a casserole, cover them and put them into a preheated 400F/200C/gas 6 oven for 25 minutes or until they are heated through. Freeze the rice in a separate container. To re-heat, wrap it in foil and put it into the oven under the meatballs.

STUFFED TOMATOES

Serves: 4
Type of dish: Hot main course
Suitable for first course: no
Preparation time: 30 minutes
Waiting time: nil
Cooking time: 25 minutes
Suitable for dinner parties: yes
Special equipment: shallow, oven-proof dish
Suitable for microwave cooking: yes
Suitable for pressure cooking: no
Suitable for freezing: yes
Calorie content: high
Carbohydrate content: medium
Fibre content: medium
Protein content: high
Fat content: medium

4 large beef tomatoes or 8 large ordinary tomatoes
3 oz (75g) wholemeal bread, without crusts
8 oz (225g) minced beef
1 oz (25g) butter
1 medium onion, finely chopped
1 garlic clove, finely chopped
1 tablespoon chopped basil, or 1 teaspoon dried
1 tablespoon chopped thyme, or 1 teaspoon dried
1 tablespoon chopped marjoram, or 1 teaspoon dried
1 tablespoon olive or sunflower oil

Cut each tomato in half lengthways. Cut away the cores. Scoop out the seeds and flesh leaving shells about ¼ inch (0.6cm) thick. Discard the seeds and chop the flesh finely. Soak the bread in a little cold water for 5 minutes.

Put the beef into a bowl. Melt the butter in a small frying pan on a low heat. Put in the onion and garlic and soften them. Mix them into the beef. Squeeze the bread dry and crumble it into the beef. Add the herbs. Mix well, squeezing the mixture together with your fingers. Mix in the chopped tomato flesh.

Pile the stuffing into the tomato shells. Use the oil to grease a shallow, ovenproof dish. Put in the tomatoes.

Bake the tomatoes for 25 minutes, or until the filling is lightly browned on top and cooked through.

Chef's tips:
☆ Serve directly from the dish.
☆ Serve with lightly cooked pasta tossed with butter and Parmesan cheese; and a green vegetable such as French beans or mange tout peas.
☆ To freeze, cool completely. Pack the tomato halves into rigid plastic containers, touching each other as little as possible. Cover them. Store for up to 1 month. Reheat from frozen. Put the tomato halves into a shallow, ovenproof dish and cover them with foil. Put them into a preheated 400F/200C/gas 6 oven for 20 minutes or until they are heated through.

STUFFED CABBAGE CASSEROLE

Serves: 4
Type of dish: Hot main course
Suitable for first course: no
1st preparation time: 40 minutes
Waiting time: nil
Cooking time: 45 minutes
2nd preparation time: 10 minutes
Suitable for dinner parties: yes
Special equipment: flameproof casserole with lid; heatproof serving dish
Suitable for microwave cooking: yes
Suitable for pressure cooking: yes
Suitable for freezing: yes
Calorie content: medium
Carbohydrate content: low
Fibre content: medium
Protein content: high
Fat content: medium

1 white cabbage, weighing 1½ - 2 lb (675 - 900g)
4 oz (125g) mushrooms
1 medium onion
2 tablespoons olive or sunflower oil
1 garlic clove, finely chopped
1 teaspoon paprika
¼ teaspoon cayenne pepper
1 lb (450g) minced beef
1 tablespoon tomato purée
2 tablespoons chopped parsley
1 tablespoon chopped thyme, or 1 teaspoon dried
4 tablespoons dry white wine or stock
1 tablespoon grated Parmesan cheese

Heat the oven to 350F/180C/gas 4.

Cut the cabbage in half lengthways and cook each half in lightly boiling salted water for 2 minutes. Drain the halves well. Run cold water over them and drain them again. Using a sharp vegetable knife, carefully scoop out the middles of the cabbage halves, leaving shells about ½ inch (1.3cm) thick. Chop all the scooped-out pieces.

Finely chop the mushrooms and the onion. Heat the oil in a large frying pan on a low heat. Stir in the onion, garlic, paprika and cayenne pepper and cook them until the onion is soft. Raise the heat and stir in the beef and mushrooms. Break the meat up well and stir until it browns. Mix in the tomato purée, herbs and wine or stock. Let the liquid boil, simmer for ½ minute and take the pan from the heat. Pile as much of this mixture as you can into the cabbage halves, mixing any left over into the chopped cabbage.

Put the chopped cabbage mixture into the bottom of a large casserole and set the stuffed cabbage halves on top. Cover the casserole and put it into the oven for 45 minutes.

Put the beef and cabbage mixture into a heatproof serving dish. Set the cabbage halves on top and sprinkle them with the cheese. Put the dish under a high grill for the cheese to brown.

☆　　☆　　☆

Chef's tips:
☆ Serve with jacket or plainly-boiled potatoes plus a root vegetable such as carrots or swede.
☆ To freeze, pack the cabbage halves and the chopped cabbage mixture into a rigid plastic

container. Reheat from frozen. Put the cabbage halves and the mixture into the casserole in which they were cooked and cover. Put into a preheated 400F / 200C / gas 6 oven for 25 minutes, or until they are heated through.

BEEF, GREEN PEA AND CARROT LOAF

Serves: 4 as a main meal; more as part of a buffet
Type of dish: Hot or cold main course
Suitable for first course: no
Preparation time: 40 minutes
Waiting time: nil
Cooking time: 40 minutes
Suitable for dinner parties: yes
Special equipment: 2 lb (900g) loaf tin
Suitable for microwave cooking: yes
Suitable for pressure cooking: no
Suitable for freezing: yes
Calorie content: high
Carbohydrate content: medium
Fibre content: medium
Protein content: high
Fat content: high

1 lb (450g) minced beef
8 oz (225g) carrots
8 oz (225g) shelled green peas (fresh or frozen)
1 medium onion
2 tablespoons olive or sunflower oil
freshly ground black pepper
½ pint (275ml) natural yoghurt
3 tablespoons chopped marjoram
1 tablespoon chopped thyme
6 tablespoons chopped parsley

Heat the oven to 350F/180C/gas 4.

Put the beef into a mixing bowl. Finely chop the carrots and boil them with the peas for 10 minutes. Drain and cool them. Finely chop the onion and soften it in the oil on a low heat.

Season the beef with the pepper and beat in 4 tablespoons of the yoghurt, 1 tablespoon of the marjoram and all the thyme. Mix in the peas, carrots and onion.

Press the mixture into a 2 lb (900g) loaf tin and smooth the top. Bake the loaf for 40 minutes, or until it is firm and brown. Turn it out of the tin. Either serve it immediately or leave it in a cool place for 2 hours to be served as a cold meal.

Make the sauce while the loaf is cooking. Put the remaining yoghurt into a blender or food processor with the remaining marjoram and the parsley. Work them together until the herbs are chopped finely and the yoghurt is a pale green colour. (*Note:* if you are using dried marjoram, make the sauce with the parsley only).

Chef's tips:

☆ Serve the loaf cut into slices with a small portion of the sauce spooned over the top. Any remaining sauce can be served separately.

☆ When cold, serve the loaf with a green salad and another based on rice, pasta or potatoes.

☆ When hot, serve with a selection of contrasting cooked vegetables such as broad beans or courgettes and either plainly boiled potatoes or potatoes that have been sliced and roasted in butter and oil.

HOT SPICED BEEF AND SWEDE LOAF

Serves: 4
Type of dish: Hot main course
Suitable for first course: no
Preparation time: 40 minutes
Waiting time: nil
Cooking time: 45 minutes
Suitable for dinner parties: yes
Special equipment: 8 inch (20cm) diameter cake
   tin with fixed base
Suitable for microwave cooking: yes
Suitable for pressure cooking: no
Suitable for freezing: yes
Calorie content: high
Carbohydrate content: medium
Fibre content: medium
Protein content: high
Fat content: high

1 lb (450g) minced beef	
1½ oz (40g) butter	
1 medium onion	
½ teaspoon cayenne pepper	
1 teaspoon paprika	
1 teaspoon ground cumin	
1 teaspoon ground coriander	
4 tablespoons stock	
1 tablespoon chopped mixed herbs	
1 tablespoon tomato purée	
1 medium swede	

Heat the oven to 350F / 180C / gas 4.

Put the beef into a bowl. Use one third of the butter to grease an 8 inch (20cm) diameter cake tin. Finely chop the onion.

Melt the remaining butter in a frying pan on a low heat. Put in the onion and soften it. Stir in the spices and continue cooking for a further 5 minutes. Add this mixture to the minced beef. Pour the stock into the frying pan and swirl it about to take up the remaining spice. Add the stock to the meat. Add the herbs and tomato purée and beat well to make a smooth mixture.

Peel the swede and cut it into thin slices. Put half of these slices into the bottom of the prepared tin in overlapping rings. Cover this with half the meat mixture. Put in all the remaining swede slices in another overlapping layer and finish with the rest of the meat. Cover the top of the tin with foil.

Put the tin on top of the stove on a medium heat for 5 minutes to brown the underneath layer of swede. Then put the tin into the oven for

45 minutes.

Turn the loaf out of the dish by first running a knife around the edges. Then invert a plate over the tin and turn both the plate and the tin over. Carefully remove the tin.

☆   ☆   ☆

Chef's tips:

☆ Serve on the plate and cut the loaf into wedges at the table.

☆ Serve with a cooked green vegetable or a green salad.

☆ To freeze, turn the loaf out of the tin and cool it completely. Wrap it in several layers of plastic film and put it into a polythene bag. To reheat, return the loaf to the tin while it is still frozen. Cover it with foil and put it into a preheated 400F/200C/gas 6 oven for 30 minutes, or until it is heated through.

MINCED BEEF AND MUSHROOM ROLL

Serves: 4
Type of dish: Hot main course
Suitable for first course: no
Preparation time: 30 minutes
Waiting time: nil
Cooking time: 30 minutes
Suitable for dinner parties: no
Special equipment: baking sheet, oven
Suitable for microwave cooking: no
Suitable for pressure cooking: no
Suitable for freezing: yes
Calorie content: high
Carbohydrate content: medium
Fibre content: medium
Protein content: high
Fat content: high

pastry:
4 oz (125g) plain flour
4 oz (125g) wholemeal flour
4 oz (125g) vegetable suet
pinch salt
1 teaspoon bicarbonate of soda
¼ pint (150ml) cold water

filling:
6 oz (175g) mushrooms
8 oz (225g) minced beef
1 garlic clove, finely chopped
6 tablespoons chopped parsley
2 tablespoons Worcestershire sauce

sauce:
2 oz (50g) mushrooms
6 spring onions
½ oz (15g) butter
1 tablespoon flour
½ pint (275ml) stock
2 tablespoons Worcestershire sauce
2 tablespoons mushroom ketchup

Heat the oven to 400F/200C/gas 6.

For the *pastry*, put the two types of flour into a bowl with the suet, salt and bicarbonate of soda. Mix them to a dough with the cold water. Leave the pastry in a cool place while you prepare the filling.

For the *filling* finely chop the mushrooms. Heat a large, heavy frying pan on a high heat without any fat. Put in the beef, break it up well and stir it until it has browned and any moisture that has collected in the pan has evaporated.

Lower the heat, mix in the garlic and mushrooms and cook for 2 minutes more, stirring. Off the heat, mix in the parsley and Worcestershire sauce.

Roll out the pastry to a rectangle about 12 inches by 15 inches (30cm by 40cm). Spread the beef filling over the surface. Roll up the pastry from one 12 inch (30cm) side. Lay the roll on a floured baking sheet.

Bake it for 25 minutes, or until it is golden brown and the surface looks slightly flaky.

Make the *sauce* while the roll is cooking. Finely chop the mushrooms and spring onions. Melt the butter in a saucepan on a low heat and cook the mushrooms and onions in it for 2 minutes. Stir in the flour and stock, raise the heat to me-

dium and stir until the sauce boils and becomes thick. Stir in the Worcestershire sauce and mushroom ketchup and simmer the sauce gently for 2 minutes.

☆   ☆   ☆

Chef's tips:
☆ Serve cut into quarter sized lengths. Serve the sauce separately.
☆ Serve with plainly-boiled potatoes and a green vegetable.
☆ To freeze, cool completely and seal in a polythene bag either whole or in short lengths. Store for up to one month. To reheat, put the roll frozen onto a floured baking sheet and put it into a preheated 400F/200C/gas 6 oven for 15 - 20 minutes.

BEEF AND BEAN PASTIES

Serves: 4
Type of dish: Hot or cold main meal or snack
Suitable for first course: no
Preparation time: 40 minutes
Waiting time: nil
Cooking time: 45 minutes
Suitable for dinner parties: no
Special equipment: baking sheet; oven
Suitable for microwave cooking: no
Suitable for pressure cooking: no
Suitable for freezing: yes
Calorie content: high
Carbohydrate content: high
Fibre content: high
Protein content: high
Fat content: medium

pastry:
4 oz (125g) plain flour
4 oz (125g) wholemeal flour
pinch salt
4 oz (125g) butter
cold water to mix
1 egg, beaten, for glaze

filling:
8 oz (225g) minced beef
4 oz (125g) potato
2 oz (50g) carrot
1 small onion
4 tablespoons chopped parsley
2 teaspoons dried mixed herbs
3 tablespoons baked beans
salt and pepper

Heat the oven to 350F/180C/gas 4. For the *pastry,* put the two types of flour into a mixing bowl with the salt. Rub in the butter and mix to a dough with cold water. Leave the pastry in a cool place while you prepare the filling.

For the *filling* put the beef into a mixing bowl. Scrub the potato but leave it unpeeled. Cut it into small, thin slivers. Cut the carrot in the same way and finely chop the onion. Add the potato, carrot and onion to the beef, together with the parsley, mixed herbs and baked beans. Season well, especially with pepper.

Divide the pastry into four equal-sized pieces. Roll each one into a circle about 7 inches (18cm) in diameter. Put one quarter of the beef mixture down the centre of each round, leaving

about 1 inch (2.5cm) space at each end. Bring the sides of the round of pastry together and seal them down the centre. Seal the ends.

Lay the finished pasties on a floured baking sheet and brush them with the beaten egg. Bake them for 45 minutes, or until they are golden brown.

☆   ☆   ☆

Chef's tips:

☆ For a hot meal, serve with a selection of cooked vegetables. No potatoes should be necessary.

☆ For a cold meal, serve with a salad.

☆ The pasties are ideal for a lunch box or picnic.

☆ To freeze, cool completely. Freeze the pasties on a tray and then pack them into polythene bags and seal them. Store for up to one month.

In the same series:

20 Ways to Cook Chicken
20 Ways to Cook Apples
20 Ways to Cook Chocolate
20 Ways to Cook Mackerel
20 Ways to Cook Cod
20 Ways to Cook Potatoes
20 Ways to Cook Soup

Others in preparation!